THE WRITER'S DATA-BOOK

The ONE Book You'll Need To Write ALL of Your Info Into!

AMBER FLORENZA

This is a WORKSHEET BOOK for fiction writers. Pages can be printed for extra characters, etc. Also, there are printable PDF worksheets available for **extra** secondary characters, extra main characters and other more. For **complete details**, please go to: amberflorenza.me.uk and follow the simple steps below:

Find your *free* PDF worksheets on amberflorenza.me.uk: Step 1) click on The Writer's Cove; Step 2) click on desired underlined link; Step 3) click on the **File button** and scroll down until you find **Print**; Step 4) print as many as you need.

ALL-AGES NONFICTION/WRITING TIPS/WORKSHEET BOOK

The Writer's Data-Book
The ONE Book You'll Need To Write ALL of Your Info Into!

ISBN-13: 978-1508601166
ISBN-10: 150860116X

A Note . . . . from Me !

Hello and *Welcome* to The Writer's Data-Book !

Instead of filling out all of the endless (but very handy and worthwhile) pages now, let's have a bit of fun! So, **Choose Your Flavor of Story!** I've made a *tasty* list below (of course, you can mix a flavor or more together--or even make up a whole new flavor yourself!). Enjoy!

- **Strawberry**: exciting, funny, always satisfying ending!
- **Vanilla**: calm, a little boring, ordinary ending.
- **Milk Chocolate**: dramatic, sweet, super ending!
- **Semi-sweet Chocolate**: unpredictable, thrilling, bittersweet ending.
- **Dark Chocolate**: mysterious, fearsome, surprise ending!
- **Pumpkin**: rich storyline, no surprises, good ending.
- **Apple**: historical, easy-to-read, typical ending.
- **Pink Grapefruit**: comedy, unromantic, somewhat cutting ending.
- **Lemon**: tear-jerker, tragic, dry-humored ending.
- **Peach**: mild, peaceful, sweet ending.
- **Orange**: sweet, fun, happy ending!
- **Ginger**: relaxing, classic, cozy ending.
- **Coconut**: harsh, complex, suspense ending.
- **Caramel**: smooth, musical, emotional ending.
- **Carrot**: spicy, melodramatic, snappy ending!
- **Oatmeal**: witty, blunt, unforgettable ending.
- **Pineapple**: provoking, sweet, healing ending.
- **Blueberry**: humorous, practical, unfinished-kind-of-ending.
- **Raspberry**: normal, light, off-the-wall ending.
- **Cinnamon**: festive, cozy-suspense, unique ending.
- **Grape**: poetic, thoughtful, effective ending.
- **Lime**: everyday, refreshing, chirpy ending!

- **Your Flavor:** _____

Best Wishes for your book,
Amber Florenza

• Book Details •

Date Your Book Begins: _____

Date Your Book Ends: _____

Choose the Flavor (or mix of flavors) of Your Story: _____

_____

Working Title of Your Book: _____

Subtitle Name (if any) : _____

Series Name (if in one) : _____

_____ Book #: _____

Exact Place: _____

Timeline(s) : _____

Major Historical Event (if any) : _____

Climax Mystery (if any) : _____

Important Landmarks: _____

Music/Tone: _____

Stores/Local Buildings: _____

_____

The Story Question: _____

Series Question (if in one) : _____

Pick A Genre (and stick to it! ☺) : _____

Reading Level/Intended Audience: _____

Circle the Word(s) You Want Your Reader To Experience At the Book's End:

Compassion | Love | Triumph | History | Joy |Healing | Power | Insight

Forgiveness | Peace | Wisdom | Hope | Faith | Strength | Truth | Humor

Patience | Equality | Purpose | Or write a word here : _____

Basic Cultural Details: _____

_____

Landscape: _____

Climate: _____

Type of Plants: _____

Main Foods Eaten: _____

Dominant Smells: _____

Type of House Main Character Lives In: _____

1-Line Purpose For Writing Book: _____

The Verse Which Your Story Surrounds:

_____

_____

_____

_____

_____

Write Your Synopsis Draft Here:

(You can revise it later)

_____

_____

_____

(The **Bold** Paragraph <u>Line</u>)

_____

_____

_____

_____

_____

_____

_____

_____

_____

_____

_____

(The Body Paragraph)

_____

_____

(The Final/Question Paragraph)

• Main Character One •

His/Her Motto: _____

Full Name: _____

Nickname(s) : _____

Hair Color/Texture: _____

Eye Color/Shape/Size: _____

Skin Color/Texture: _____

Height: _____ Weight (approx) : _____

Age: _____ Birthday/Year Born: _____

Birthplace: _____ Nationality: _____

Second Language(s) (if any) : _____

Describe His/Her Voice: _____

Attitude About Life: _____

Dress Style(s) : _____

Strengths: _____

Weaknesses: _____

Fears: _____

Dreams: _____

Hopes: _____

Peeves: _____

Flaws: _____

Abilities: _____

Accomplishments: _____

Misfortunes: _____

Desire To Accomplish: _____

Values: _____

Motivation: _____

Interests: _____

Hobbies: _____

Occupation (either job title or position such as: student, wife, grandmother,

retired, etc) : _____

Eating Habits: _____

Sleeping Habits: _____

Everyday Habits: _____

Vehicles (he/she drives in) : _____

_____

Reaction To Danger: _____

Reaction To Emergency: _____

Reaction To Compliments: _____

Reaction To Pain: _____

Reaction To Fear: _____

Reaction To Disappointments: _____

Reaction To Success: _____

Reaction To His/Her Climate: _____

Favorite Climate/Weather: _____

Allergic To... (examples: dust, work) : _____

Favorite Foods/Drinks: _____

_____

Foods/Drinks That Don't Go Down Well: _____

_____

Favorite Thing To Do: _____

Worst Thing To Do: _____

Pet(s), if any: _____

Favorite Animal(s) : _____

Regional Animals: _____

Reaction To Animals: _____

Favorite Memory: _____

_____

Worst Memory: _____

_____

Most Embarrassing Memory: _____

_____

Most Elated Memory: _____

_____

Physical Journey: _____

_____

Spiritual Journey: _____

_____

Brief Personal History: _____

_____

_____

_____

_____

Brief Family History: _____

_____

_____

_____

_____

Background (write a few events that has *just happened* before the book begins, that will shape the story) : _____

_____

_____

_____

_____

His/Her Favorite Verse:

_____

_____

_____

_____

_____

_____

• THE (SIMPLE) FAMILY TREE •

```
        _____
                |        |  _____
                |        |    (spouse, if one)
                |
                |
Father _____ & _____ Mother
               |                  |
(Father's _____    _____ (Mother's
          &                         &
parents) _____    _____ parents)
```

LIST OF FAMILY/FRIENDS (names only) :

Children (if any) : _____   _____

_____   _____

Spouse's Parents and Grandparents (if married) :

_____   _____

_____   _____

Siblings: _____   _____

_____   _____

_____   _____

Uncles, Aunts & Cousins: _____   _____

_____   _____   _____

_____   _____   _____

_____   _____   _____

_____   _____   _____

_____   _____   _____

In-Laws (if married) : _____   _____

_____   _____   _____

_____   _____   _____

_____   _____   _____

_____   _____   _____

Best/Closest Friend(s) : _____   _____

_____   _____   _____

_____   _____   _____

_____   _____   _____

Historical Characters (if any) : _____ : _____

_____ : _____ : _____

Inspiring Person(s) : _____   _____

_____   _____   _____

• Main Character Two •

Her/His Motto: _____

Full Name: _____

Nickname(s) : _____

Hair Color/Texture: _____

Eye Color/Shape/Size: _____

Skin Color/Texture: _____

Height: _____ Weight (approx) : _____

Age: _____ Birthday/Year Born: _____

Birthplace: _____ Nationality: _____

Second Language(s) (if any) : _____

Describe Her/His Voice: _____

Attitude About Life: _____

Dress Style(s) : _____

Strengths: _____

Weaknesses: _____

Fears: _____

Dreams: _____

Hopes: _____

Peeves: _____

Flaws: _____

Abilities: _____

Accomplishments: _____

Misfortunes: _____

Desire To Accomplish: _____

Values: _____

Motivation: _____

Interests: _____

Hobbies: _____

Occupation (either job title or position such as: student, wife, grandmother,

retired, etc) : _____

Eating Habits: _____

Sleeping Habits: _____

Everyday Habits: _____

Vehicles (she/he drives in) : _____

_____

Reaction To Danger: _____

Reaction To Emergency: _____

Reaction To Compliments: _____

Reaction To Pain: _____

Reaction To Fear: _____

Reaction To Disappointments: _____

Reaction To Success: _____

Reaction To Her/His Climate: _____

Favorite Climate/Weather: _____

Allergic To… (examples: dust, work) : _____

Favorite Foods/Drinks: _____

_____

Foods/Drinks That Don't Go Down Well: _____

_____

Favorite Thing To Do: _____

Worst Thing To Do: _____

Pet(s), if any: _____

Favorite Animal(s) : _____

Regional Animals: _____

Reaction To Animals: _____

Favorite Memory: _____

_____

Worst Memory: _____

_____

Most Embarrassing Memory: _____

_____

Most Elated Memory: _____

_____

Physical Journey: _____

_____

Spiritual Journey: _____

_____

Brief Personal History: _____

_____

_____

_____

_____

Brief Family History: _____

_____

_____

_____

_____

Background (write a few events that has *just happened* before the book begins, that will shape the story) : _____

_____

_____

_____

_____

His/Her Favorite Verse:

_____

_____

_____

_____

_____

_____

• THE (SIMPLE) FAMILY TREE •

```
           _____
              |         |  _____
              |         |
              |            (spouse, if one)
              |
Father _____  & _____  Mother
              |                    |
(Father's _____      _____  (Mother's
          &                         &
parents) _____      _____  parents)
```

LIST OF FAMILY/FRIENDS (names only) :

Children (if any) : _____   _____

                    _____   _____

Spouse's Parents and Grandparents (if married) :

_____   _____

_____   _____

Siblings: _____   _____

_____   _____

_____   _____

Uncles, Aunts & Cousins: _____ _____

_____ _____ _____

_____ _____ _____

_____ _____ _____

_____ _____ _____

_____ _____ _____

In-Laws (if married) :   _____ _____

_____ _____ _____

_____ _____ _____

_____ _____ _____

_____ _____ _____

Best/Closest Friend(s) :   _____ _____

_____ _____ _____

_____ _____ _____

_____ _____ _____

Historical Characters (if any) : _____:_____

_____:_____:_____

Inspiring Person(s) : _____   _____

_____ _____ _____

• Secondary Character Who Matters •

Full Name: _____

Circle the Relation To Main Character:

Family | Friend | Foe | Neighbor | Other

Hair Color/Texture: _____

Eye Color/Shape/Size: _____

Skin Color/Texture: _____ Height: _____ Build : _____

Age: _____ Birthday/Year Born: _____

Describe His/Her Voice: _____

Attitude About Life: _____

Dress Style(s) : _____

What He/She Thinks of Main Character: _____

_____

What Main Character Thinks of Him/Her: _____

_____

Strengths: _____

Weaknesses: _____

Fears: _____

Dreams: _____

Hopes: _____

Peeves: _____

Flaws: _____

Abilities: _____

Accomplishments: _____

Misfortunes: _____

Desire To Accomplish: _____

Values: _____

Motivation: _____

Interests: _____

Hobbies: _____

Occupation (either job title or position such as: student, wife, grandmother,

retired, etc) : _____

Eating Habits: _____

Sleeping Habits: _____

Everyday Habits: _____

Vehicles (she/he drives in) : _____

_____

Reaction To Danger: _____

Reaction To Emergency: _____

Reaction To Compliments: _____

Reaction To Pain: _____

Reaction To Fear: _____

Reaction To Disappointments: _____

Reaction To Success: _____

Reaction To His/Her Climate: _____

Favorite Climate/Weather: _____

Allergic To... (examples: dust, work) : _____

Favorite Foods/Drinks: _____

_____

Foods/Drinks That Don't Go Down Well: _____

_____

Favorite Thing To Do: _____

Worst Thing To Do: _____

Pet(s), if any: _____

Reaction To Animals: _____

Favorite Memory: _____

_____

Worst Memory: _____

_____

Most Embarrassing Memory: _____

_____

Most Elated Memory: _____

_____

Brief Personal History: _____

_____

_____

_____

What Role Does He/She Play In Book? _____

• Secondary Character Who Matters •

Full Name: _____

Circle the Relation To Main Character:

Family | Friend | Foe | Neighbor | Other

Hair Color/Texture: _____

Eye Color/Shape/Size: _____

Skin Color/Texture: _____ Height: _____ Build : _____

Age: _____ Birthday/Year Born: _____

Describe His/Her Voice: _____

Attitude About Life: _____

Dress Style(s) : _____

What He/She Thinks of Main Character: _____

_____

What Main Character Thinks of Him/Her: _____

_____

Strengths: _____

Weaknesses: _____

Fears: _____

Dreams: _____

Hopes: _____

Peeves: _____

Flaws: _____

Abilities: _____

Accomplishments: _____

Misfortunes: _____

Desire To Accomplish: _____

Values: _____

Motivation: _____

Interests: _____

Hobbies: _____

Occupation (either job title or position such as: student, wife, grandmother,

retired, etc) : _____

Eating Habits: _____

Sleeping Habits: _____

Everyday Habits: _____

Vehicles (she/he drives in) : _____

_____

Reaction To Danger: _____

Reaction To Emergency: _____

Reaction To Compliments: _____

Reaction To Pain: _____

Reaction To Fear: _____

Reaction To Disappointments: _____

Reaction To Success: _____

Reaction To His/Her Climate: _____

Favorite Climate/Weather: _____

Allergic To... (examples: dust, work) : _____

Favorite Foods/Drinks: _____

_____

Foods/Drinks That Don't Go Down Well: _____

_____

Favorite Thing To Do: _____

Worst Thing To Do: _____

Pet(s), if any: _____

Reaction To Animals: _____

Favorite Memory: _____

_____

Worst Memory: _____

_____

Most Embarrassing Memory: _____

_____

Most Elated Memory: _____

_____

Brief Personal History: _____

_____

_____

_____

What Role Does He/She Play In Book? _____

• Secondary Character Who Matters •

Full Name: _____

Circle the Relation To Main Character:

Family | Friend | Foe | Neighbor | Other

Hair Color/Texture: _____

Eye Color/Shape/Size: _____

Skin Color/Texture: _____ Height: _____ Build : _____

Age: _____ Birthday/Year Born: _____

Describe His/Her Voice: _____

Attitude About Life: _____

Dress Style(s) : _____

What He/She Thinks of Main Character: _____

_____

What Main Character Thinks of Him/Her: _____

_____

Strengths: _____

Weaknesses: _____

Fears: _____

Dreams: _____

Hopes: _____

Peeves: _____

Flaws: _____

Abilities: _____

Accomplishments: _____

Misfortunes: _____

Desire To Accomplish: _____

Values: _____

Motivation: _____

Interests: _____

Hobbies: _____

Occupation (either job title or position such as: student, wife, grandmother, retired, etc) : _____

Eating Habits: _____

Sleeping Habits: _____

Everyday Habits: _____

Vehicles (she/he drives in) : _____

_____

Reaction To Danger: _____

Reaction To Emergency: _____

Reaction To Compliments: _____

Reaction To Pain: _____

Reaction To Fear: _____

Reaction To Disappointments: _____

Reaction To Success: _____

Reaction To His/Her Climate: _____

Favorite Climate/Weather: _____

Allergic To... (examples: dust, work) : _____

Favorite Foods/Drinks: _____

_____

Foods/Drinks That Don't Go Down Well: _____

_____

Favorite Thing To Do: _____

Worst Thing To Do: _____

Pet(s), if any: _____

Reaction To Animals: _____

Favorite Memory: _____

_____

Worst Memory: _____

_____

Most Embarrassing Memory: _____

_____

Most Elated Memory: _____

_____

Brief Personal History: _____

_____

_____

_____

What Role Does He/She Play In Book? _____

• Secondary Character Who Matters •

Full Name: _____

Circle the Relation To Main Character:

Family | Friend | Foe | Neighbor | Other

Hair Color/Texture: _____

Eye Color/Shape/Size: _____

Skin Color/Texture: _____ Height: _____ Build : _____

Age: _____ Birthday/Year Born: _____

Describe His/Her Voice: _____

Attitude About Life: _____

Dress Style(s) : _____

What He/She Thinks of Main Character: _____

_____

What Main Character Thinks of Him/Her: _____

_____

Strengths: _____

Weaknesses: _____

Fears: _____

Dreams: _____

Hopes: _____

Peeves: _____

Flaws: _____

Abilities: _____

Accomplishments: _____

Misfortunes: _____

Desire To Accomplish: _____

Values: _____

Motivation: _____

Interests: _____

Hobbies: _____

Occupation (either job title or position such as: student, wife, grandmother,

retired, etc) : _____

Eating Habits: _____

Sleeping Habits: _____

Everyday Habits: _____

Vehicles (she/he drives in) : _____

_____

Reaction To Danger: _____

Reaction To Emergency: _____

Reaction To Compliments: _____

Reaction To Pain: _____

Reaction To Fear: _____

Reaction To Disappointments: _____

Reaction To Success: _____

Reaction To His/Her Climate: _____

Favorite Climate/Weather: _____

Allergic To... (examples: dust, work) : _____

Favorite Foods/Drinks: _____

_____

Foods/Drinks That Don't Go Down Well: _____

_____

Favorite Thing To Do: _____

Worst Thing To Do: _____

Pet(s), if any: _____

Reaction To Animals: _____

Favorite Memory: _____

_____

Worst Memory: _____

_____

Most Embarrassing Memory: _____

_____

Most Elated Memory: _____

_____

Brief Personal History: _____

_____

_____

_____

What Role Does He/She Play In Book? _____

• Secondary Character Who Matters •

Full Name: _____

Circle the Relation To Main Character:

Family | Friend | Foe | Neighbor | Other

Hair Color/Texture: _____

Eye Color/Shape/Size: _____

Skin Color/Texture: _____ Height: _____ Build : _____

Age: _____ Birthday/Year Born: _____

Describe His/Her Voice: _____

Attitude About Life: _____

Dress Style(s) : _____

What He/She Thinks of Main Character: _____

_____

What Main Character Thinks of Him/Her: _____

_____

Strengths: _____

Weaknesses: _____

Fears: _____

Dreams: _____

Hopes: _____

Peeves: _____

Flaws: _____

Abilities: _____

Accomplishments: _____

Misfortunes: _____

Desire To Accomplish: _____

Values: _____

Motivation: _____

Interests: _____

Hobbies: _____

Occupation (either job title or position such as: student, wife, grandmother,

retired, etc) : _____

Eating Habits: _____

Sleeping Habits: _____

Everyday Habits: _____

Vehicles (she/he drives in) : _____

_____

Reaction To Danger: _____

Reaction To Emergency: _____

Reaction To Compliments: _____

Reaction To Pain: _____

Reaction To Fear: _____

Reaction To Disappointments: _____

Reaction To Success: _____

Reaction To His/Her Climate: _____

Favorite Climate/Weather: _____

Allergic To... (examples: dust, work) : _____

Favorite Foods/Drinks: _____

_____

Foods/Drinks That Don't Go Down Well: _____

_____

Favorite Thing To Do: _____

Worst Thing To Do: _____

Pet(s), if any: _____

Reaction To Animals: _____

Favorite Memory: _____

_____

Worst Memory: _____

_____

Most Embarrassing Memory: _____

_____

Most Elated Memory: _____

_____

Brief Personal History: _____

_____

_____

_____

What Role Does He/She Play In Book? _____

• Secondary Character Who Matters •

Full Name: _____

Circle the Relation To Main Character:

Family | Friend | Foe | Neighbor | Other

Hair Color/Texture: _____

Eye Color/Shape/Size: _____

Skin Color/Texture: _____ Height: _____ Build : _____

Age: _____ Birthday/Year Born: _____

Describe His/Her Voice: _____

Attitude About Life: _____

Dress Style(s) : _____

What He/She Thinks of Main Character: _____

_____

What Main Character Thinks of Him/Her: _____

_____

Strengths: _____

Weaknesses: _____

Fears: _____

Dreams: _____

Hopes: _____

Peeves: _____

Flaws: _____

Abilities: _____

Accomplishments: _____

Misfortunes: _____

Desire To Accomplish: _____

Values: _____

Motivation: _____

Interests: _____

Hobbies: _____

Occupation (either job title or position such as: student, wife, grandmother,

retired, etc) : _____

Eating Habits: _____

Sleeping Habits: _____

Everyday Habits: _____

Vehicles (she/he drives in) : _____

_____

Reaction To Danger: _____

Reaction To Emergency: _____

Reaction To Compliments: _____

Reaction To Pain: _____

Reaction To Fear: _____

Reaction To Disappointments: _____

Reaction To Success: _____

Reaction To His/Her Climate: _____

Favorite Climate/Weather: _____

Allergic To... (examples: dust, work) : _____

Favorite Foods/Drinks: _____

_____

Foods/Drinks That Don't Go Down Well: _____

_____

Favorite Thing To Do: _____

Worst Thing To Do: _____

Pet(s), if any: _____

Reaction To Animals: _____

Favorite Memory: _____

_____

Worst Memory: _____

_____

Most Embarrassing Memory: _____

_____

Most Elated Memory: _____

_____

Brief Personal History: _____

_____

_____

_____

What Role Does He/She Play In Book? _____

• Secondary Character Who Matters •

Full Name: _____

Circle the Relation To Main Character:

Family | Friend | Foe | Neighbor | Other

Hair Color/Texture: _____

Eye Color/Shape/Size: _____

Skin Color/Texture: _____ Height: _____ Build : _____

Age: _____ Birthday/Year Born: _____

Describe His/Her Voice: _____

Attitude About Life: _____

Dress Style(s) : _____

What He/She Thinks of Main Character: _____

_____

What Main Character Thinks of Him/Her: _____

_____

Strengths: _____

Weaknesses: _____

Fears: _____

Dreams: _____

Hopes: _____

Peeves: _____

Flaws: _____

Abilities: _____

Accomplishments: _____

Misfortunes: _____

Desire To Accomplish: _____

Values: _____

Motivation: _____

Interests: _____

Hobbies: _____

Occupation (either job title or position such as: student, wife, grandmother,

retired, etc) : _____

Eating Habits: _____

Sleeping Habits: _____

Everyday Habits: _____

Vehicles (she/he drives in) : _____

_____

Reaction To Danger: _____

Reaction To Emergency: _____

Reaction To Compliments: _____

Reaction To Pain: _____

Reaction To Fear: _____

Reaction To Disappointments: _____

Reaction To Success: _____

Reaction To His/Her Climate: _____

Favorite Climate/Weather: _____

Allergic To... (examples: dust, work) : _____

Favorite Foods/Drinks: _____

_____

Foods/Drinks That Don't Go Down Well: _____

_____

Favorite Thing To Do: _____

Worst Thing To Do: _____

Pet(s), if any: _____

Reaction To Animals: _____

Favorite Memory: _____

_____

Worst Memory: _____

_____

Most Embarrassing Memory: _____

_____

Most Elated Memory: _____

_____

Brief Personal History: _____

_____

_____

_____

What Role Does He/She Play In Book? _____

• Secondary Character Who Matters •

Full Name: _____

Circle the Relation To Main Character:

Family | Friend | Foe | Neighbor | Other

Hair Color/Texture: _____

Eye Color/Shape/Size: _____

Skin Color/Texture: _____ Height: _____ Build : _____

Age: _____ Birthday/Year Born: _____

Describe His/Her Voice: _____

Attitude About Life: _____

Dress Style(s) : _____

What He/She Thinks of Main Character: _____

_____

What Main Character Thinks of Him/Her: _____

_____

Strengths: _____

Weaknesses: _____

Fears: _____

Dreams: _____

Hopes: _____

Peeves: _____

Flaws: _____

Abilities: _____

Accomplishments: _____

Misfortunes: _____

Desire To Accomplish: _____

Values: _____

Motivation: _____

Interests: _____

Hobbies: _____

Occupation (either job title or position such as: student, wife, grandmother,

retired, etc) : _____

Eating Habits: _____

Sleeping Habits: _____

Everyday Habits: _____

Vehicles (she/he drives in) : _____

_____

Reaction To Danger: _____

Reaction To Emergency: _____

Reaction To Compliments: _____

Reaction To Pain: _____

Reaction To Fear: _____

Reaction To Disappointments: _____

Reaction To Success: _____

Reaction To His/Her Climate: _____

Favorite Climate/Weather: _____

Allergic To... (examples: dust, work) : _____

Favorite Foods/Drinks: _____

_____

Foods/Drinks That Don't Go Down Well: _____

_____

Favorite Thing To Do: _____

Worst Thing To Do: _____

Pet(s), if any: _____

Reaction To Animals: _____

Favorite Memory: _____

_____

Worst Memory: _____

_____

Most Embarrassing Memory: _____

_____

Most Elated Memory: _____

_____

Brief Personal History: _____

_____

_____

_____

What Role Does He/She Play In Book? _____

• Secondary Character Who Matters •

Full Name: _____

Circle the Relation To Main Character:

Family | Friend | Foe | Neighbor | Other

Hair Color/Texture: _____

Eye Color/Shape/Size: _____

Skin Color/Texture: _____ Height: _____ Build : _____

Age: _____ Birthday/Year Born: _____

Describe His/Her Voice: _____

Attitude About Life: _____

Dress Style(s) : _____

What He/She Thinks of Main Character: _____

_____

What Main Character Thinks of Him/Her: _____

_____

Strengths: _____

Weaknesses: _____

Fears: _____

Dreams: _____

Hopes: _____

Peeves: _____

Flaws: _____

Abilities: _____

Accomplishments: _____

Misfortunes: _____

Desire To Accomplish: _____

Values: _____

Motivation: _____

Interests: _____

Hobbies: _____

Occupation (either job title or position such as: student, wife, grandmother,

retired, etc) : _____

Eating Habits: _____

Sleeping Habits: _____

Everyday Habits: _____

Vehicles (she/he drives in) : _____

_____

Reaction To Danger: _____

Reaction To Emergency: _____

Reaction To Compliments: _____

Reaction To Pain: _____

Reaction To Fear: _____

Reaction To Disappointments: _____

Reaction To Success: _____

Reaction To His/Her Climate: _____

Favorite Climate/Weather: _____

Allergic To... (examples: dust, work) : _____

Favorite Foods/Drinks: _____

_____

Foods/Drinks That Don't Go Down Well: _____

_____

Favorite Thing To Do: _____

Worst Thing To Do: _____

Pet(s), if any: _____

Reaction To Animals: _____

Favorite Memory: _____

_____

Worst Memory: _____

_____

Most Embarrassing Memory: _____

_____

Most Elated Memory: _____

_____

Brief Personal History: _____

_____

_____

_____

What Role Does He/She Play In Book? _____

• Secondary Character Who Matters •

Full Name: _____

Circle the Relation To Main Character:

Family | Friend | Foe | Neighbor | Other

Hair Color/Texture: _____

Eye Color/Shape/Size: _____

Skin Color/Texture: _____ Height: _____ Build : _____

Age: _____ Birthday/Year Born: _____

Describe His/Her Voice: _____

Attitude About Life: _____

Dress Style(s) : _____

What He/She Thinks of Main Character: _____

_____

What Main Character Thinks of Him/Her: _____

_____

Strengths: _____

Weaknesses: _____

Fears: _____

Dreams: _____

Hopes: _____

Peeves: _____

Flaws: _____

Abilities: _____

Accomplishments: _____

Misfortunes: _____

Desire To Accomplish: _____

Values: _____

Motivation: _____

Interests: _____

Hobbies: _____

Occupation (either job title or position such as: student, wife, grandmother,

retired, etc) : _____

Eating Habits: _____

Sleeping Habits: _____

Everyday Habits: _____

Vehicles (she/he drives in) : _____

_____

Reaction To Danger: _____

Reaction To Emergency: _____

Reaction To Compliments: _____

Reaction To Pain: _____

Reaction To Fear: _____

Reaction To Disappointments: _____

Reaction To Success: _____

Reaction To His/Her Climate: _____

Favorite Climate/Weather: _____

Allergic To... (examples: dust, work) : _____

Favorite Foods/Drinks: _____

_____

Foods/Drinks That Don't Go Down Well: _____

_____

Favorite Thing To Do: _____

Worst Thing To Do: _____

Pet(s), if any: _____

Reaction To Animals: _____

Favorite Memory: _____

_____

Worst Memory: _____

_____

Most Embarrassing Memory: _____

_____

Most Elated Memory: _____

_____

Brief Personal History: _____

_____

_____

_____

What Role Does He/She Play In Book? _____

• Secondary Character Who Exists •

Full Name: _____

Circle the Relation To Main Character:

Family | Friend | Foe | Neighbor | Other

Hair Color/Texture: _____

Eye Color/Shape/Size: _____

Skin Color/Texture: _____ Weight/Build : _____

Height: _____ Age : ____ Birthday/Year Born: _____

Describe Her/His Voice: _____

Dress Style(s) : _____

Attitude Towards Main Character: _____

Main Character's Attitude of Him/Her: _____

Strengths: _____

Weaknesses: _____

Fears: _____

Flaws: _____

Abilities: _____

Accomplishments: _____

Misfortunes: _____

Values: _____

Motivation: _____

Occupation (either job title or position such as: student, wife, grandmother,

retired, etc) : _____

Vehicles (she/he drives in) : _____

_____

Reaction To Danger: _____

Reaction To Emergency: _____

Reaction To His/Her Climate: _____

Favorite Thing To Do: _____

Worst Thing To Do: _____

Pet(s), if any: _____

Reaction To Animals: _____

Brief Personal History: _____

_____

_____

_____

What Role Does He/She Play In Book? _____

• Secondary Character Who Exists •

Full Name: _____

Circle the Relation To Main Character:

Family | Friend | Foe | Neighbor | Other

Hair Color/Texture: _____

Eye Color/Shape/Size: _____

Skin Color/Texture: _____ Weight/Build : _____

Height: _____ Age : ____ Birthday/Year Born: _____

Describe Her/His Voice: _____

Dress Style(s) : _____

Attitude Towards Main Character: _____

Main Character's Attitude of Him/Her: _____

Strengths: _____

Weaknesses: _____

Fears: _____

Flaws: _____

Abilities: _____

Accomplishments: _____

Misfortunes: _____

Values: _____

Motivation: _____

Occupation (either job title or position such as: student, wife, grandmother, retired, etc) : _____

Vehicles (she/he drives in) : _____

_____

Reaction To Danger: _____

Reaction To Emergency: _____

Reaction To His/Her Climate: _____

Favorite Thing To Do: _____

Worst Thing To Do: _____

Pet(s), if any: _____

Reaction To Animals: _____

Brief Personal History: _____

_____

_____

_____

What Role Does He/She Play In Book? _____

• Secondary Character Who Exists •

Full Name: _____

Circle the Relation To Main Character:

Family | Friend | Foe | Neighbor | Other

Hair Color/Texture: _____

Eye Color/Shape/Size: _____

Skin Color/Texture: _____ Weight/Build : _____

Height: _____ Age : ____ Birthday/Year Born: _____

Describe Her/His Voice: _____

Dress Style(s) : _____

Attitude Towards Main Character: _____

Main Character's Attitude of Him/Her: _____

Strengths: _____

Weaknesses: _____

Fears: _____

Flaws: _____

Abilities: _____

Accomplishments: _____

Misfortunes: _____

Values: _____

Motivation: _____

Occupation (either job title or position such as: student, wife, grandmother, retired, etc) : _____

Vehicles (she/he drives in) : _____

_____

Reaction To Danger: _____

Reaction To Emergency: _____

Reaction To His/Her Climate: _____

Favorite Thing To Do: _____

Worst Thing To Do: _____

Pet(s), if any: _____

Reaction To Animals: _____

Brief Personal History: _____

_____

_____

_____

What Role Does He/She Play In Book? _____

• Secondary Character Who Exists •

Full Name: _____

Circle the Relation To Main Character:

Family | Friend | Foe | Neighbor | Other

Hair Color/Texture: _____

Eye Color/Shape/Size: _____

Skin Color/Texture: _____ Weight/Build : _____

Height: _____ Age : _____ Birthday/Year Born: _____

Describe Her/His Voice: _____

Dress Style(s) : _____

Attitude Towards Main Character: _____

Main Character's Attitude of Him/Her: _____

Strengths: _____

Weaknesses: _____

Fears: _____

Flaws: _____

Abilities: _____

Accomplishments: _____

Misfortunes: _____

Values: _____

Motivation: _____

Occupation (either job title or position such as: student, wife, grandmother, retired, etc) : _____

Vehicles (she/he drives in) : _____

_____

Reaction To Danger: _____

Reaction To Emergency: _____

Reaction To His/Her Climate: _____

Favorite Thing To Do: _____

Worst Thing To Do: _____

Pet(s), if any: _____

Reaction To Animals: _____

Brief Personal History: _____

_____

_____

_____

What Role Does He/She Play In Book? _____

• Secondary Character Who Exists •

Full Name: _____

Circle the Relation To Main Character:

Family | Friend | Foe | Neighbor | Other

Hair Color/Texture: _____

Eye Color/Shape/Size: _____

Skin Color/Texture: _____ Weight/Build : _____

Height: _____ Age : _____ Birthday/Year Born: _____

Describe Her/His Voice: _____

Dress Style(s) : _____

Attitude Towards Main Character: _____

Main Character's Attitude of Him/Her: _____

Strengths: _____

Weaknesses: _____

Fears: _____

Flaws: _____

Abilities: _____

Accomplishments: _____

Misfortunes: _____

Values: _____

Motivation: _____

Occupation (either job title or position such as: student, wife, grandmother,

retired, etc) : _____

Vehicles (she/he drives in) : _____

_____

Reaction To Danger: _____

Reaction To Emergency: _____

Reaction To His/Her Climate: _____

Favorite Thing To Do: _____

Worst Thing To Do: _____

Pet(s), if any: _____

Reaction To Animals: _____

Brief Personal History: _____

_____

_____

_____

What Role Does He/She Play In Book? _____

• Secondary Character Who Exists •

Full Name: _____

Circle the Relation To Main Character:

Family | Friend | Foe | Neighbor | Other

Hair Color/Texture: _____

Eye Color/Shape/Size: _____

Skin Color/Texture: _____ Weight/Build : _____

Height: _____ Age : _____ Birthday/Year Born: _____

Describe Her/His Voice: _____

Dress Style(s) : _____

Attitude Towards Main Character: _____

Main Character's Attitude of Him/Her: _____

Strengths: _____

Weaknesses: _____

Fears: _____

Flaws: _____

Abilities: _____

Accomplishments: _____

Misfortunes: _____

Values: _____

Motivation: _____

Occupation (either job title or position such as: student, wife, grandmother, retired, etc) : _____

Vehicles (she/he drives in) : _____

_____

Reaction To Danger: _____

Reaction To Emergency: _____

Reaction To His/Her Climate: _____

Favorite Thing To Do: _____

Worst Thing To Do: _____

Pet(s), if any: _____

Reaction To Animals: _____

Brief Personal History: _____

_____

_____

_____

What Role Does He/She Play In Book? _____

• Secondary Character Who Exists •

Full Name: _____

Circle the Relation To Main Character:

Family | Friend | Foe | Neighbor | Other

Hair Color/Texture: _____

Eye Color/Shape/Size: _____

Skin Color/Texture: _____ Weight/Build : _____

Height: _____ Age : _____ Birthday/Year Born: _____

Describe Her/His Voice: _____

Dress Style(s) : _____

Attitude Towards Main Character: _____

Main Character's Attitude of Him/Her: _____

Strengths: _____

Weaknesses: _____

Fears: _____

Flaws: _____

Abilities: _____

Accomplishments: _____

Misfortunes: _____

Values: _____

Motivation: _____

Occupation (either job title or position such as: student, wife, grandmother, retired, etc) : _____

Vehicles (she/he drives in) : _____

_____

Reaction To Danger: _____

Reaction To Emergency: _____

Reaction To His/Her Climate: _____

Favorite Thing To Do: _____

Worst Thing To Do: _____

Pet(s), if any: _____

Reaction To Animals: _____

Brief Personal History: _____

_____

_____

_____

What Role Does He/She Play In Book? _____

• Secondary Character Who Exists •

Full Name: _____

Circle the Relation To Main Character:

Family | Friend | Foe | Neighbor | Other

Hair Color/Texture: _____

Eye Color/Shape/Size: _____

Skin Color/Texture: _____ Weight/Build : _____

Height: _____ Age : _____ Birthday/Year Born: _____

Describe Her/His Voice: _____

Dress Style(s) : _____

Attitude Towards Main Character: _____

Main Character's Attitude of Him/Her: _____

Strengths: _____

Weaknesses: _____

Fears: _____

Flaws: _____

Abilities: _____

Accomplishments: _____

Misfortunes: _____

Values: _____

Motivation: _____

Occupation (either job title or position such as: student, wife, grandmother, retired, etc) : _____

Vehicles (she/he drives in) : _____

_____

Reaction To Danger: _____

Reaction To Emergency: _____

Reaction To His/Her Climate: _____

Favorite Thing To Do: _____

Worst Thing To Do: _____

Pet(s), if any: _____

Reaction To Animals: _____

Brief Personal History: _____

_____

_____

_____

What Role Does He/She Play In Book? _____

• Secondary Character Who Exists •

Full Name: _____

Circle the Relation To Main Character:

Family | Friend | Foe | Neighbor | Other

Hair Color/Texture: _____

Eye Color/Shape/Size: _____

Skin Color/Texture: _____ Weight/Build : _____

Height: _____ Age : _____ Birthday/Year Born: _____

Describe Her/His Voice: _____

Dress Style(s) : _____

Attitude Towards Main Character: _____

Main Character's Attitude of Him/Her: _____

Strengths: _____

Weaknesses: _____

Fears: _____

Flaws: _____

Abilities: _____

Accomplishments: _____

Misfortunes: _____

Values: _____

Motivation: _____

Occupation (either job title or position such as: student, wife, grandmother, retired, etc) : _____

Vehicles (she/he drives in) : _____

_____

Reaction To Danger: _____

Reaction To Emergency: _____

Reaction To His/Her Climate: _____

Favorite Thing To Do: _____

Worst Thing To Do: _____

Pet(s), if any: _____

Reaction To Animals: _____

Brief Personal History: _____

_____

_____

_____

What Role Does He/She Play In Book? _____

• Secondary Character Who Exists •

Full Name: _____

Circle the Relation To Main Character:

Family | Friend | Foe | Neighbor | Other

Hair Color/Texture: _____

Eye Color/Shape/Size: _____

Skin Color/Texture: _____ Weight/Build : _____

Height: _____ Age : _____ Birthday/Year Born: _____

Describe Her/His Voice: _____

Dress Style(s) : _____

Attitude Towards Main Character: _____

Main Character's Attitude of Him/Her: _____

Strengths: _____

Weaknesses: _____

Fears: _____

Flaws: _____

Abilities: _____

Accomplishments: _____

Misfortunes: _____

Values: _____

Motivation: _____

Occupation (either job title or position such as: student, wife, grandmother, retired, etc) : _____

Vehicles (she/he drives in) : _____

_____

Reaction To Danger: _____

Reaction To Emergency: _____

Reaction To His/Her Climate: _____

Favorite Thing To Do: _____

Worst Thing To Do: _____

Pet(s), if any: _____

Reaction To Animals: _____

Brief Personal History: _____

_____

_____

_____

What Role Does He/She Play In Book? _____

DIAGRAM YOUR MAIN CHARACTER'S HOUSE! (Draw Freehand Below) :

SKETCH FLOOR PLANS OF IMPORTANT PLACES (optional but very handy) :

AND NOW THAT YOUR HOMEWORK IS DONE . . . IT'S TIME TO WRITE THAT BOOK! ☺

Printed in Great Britain
by Amazon